Tasha

My Story

By Paula Emery

Paula Emery is a fine artist whose work reflects her love of animals and their unique personalities, and the wonder and beauty of the natural world. She is an artist, writer and gardener who lives in the rural countryside of Connecticut.

A late spring rain had just ended when I heard a loud piercing, mournful cry. It went on and on. My son and I went outside, searching for the source. There in the field lay a newborn deer - all alone and not yet able to walk. It is here the story of Tasha begins.....

...The story of an abandoned fawn. She was unable to walk and cried in despair - hungry, cold and alone. I tried to feed Tasha some milk but she wouldn't lick if from my finger nor drink from a turkey baster.

When we realized this wasn't working, we asked ourselves "what do we do now"?

We brought Tasha to a local sheep farmer who gave her the colostrum she needed to live. She should have received this from her own mother's milk, but instead, this lifesaving nutrient came from a mother sheep who had just given birth.

The sheep farmer explained that it was highly unlikely for a fawn this small to survive in captivity - but she gave us a special bottle, a supply of sheep's milk and well wishes.

The sheep farmer also told us that even if she lived, it would be highly unlikely that the fawn could ever readapt to the wild. Our new challenge - to keep Tasha alive - and get her back into her "natural world...when the "time" came.

Tasha had to be fed by bottle

every four hours.

Soon she slept through the night after her 11:00 feeding.

The fawn befriended Morgan, our laid back cocker dog and the cats, Arthur, Avalon and Leo. They accepted Tasha immediately... like a new stray from the pound.

Who wants to cuddle or who wants to play? Will it be hide and go seek? Or cat - fawn stare down? Or would you like to take a nap with me?

Tasha learned to drink "yummy" sheep's milk from a bottle.

Even in the house, we announce mealtime for Tasha by ringing a

bell - knowing that she will not always be an indoor "pet".

Tasha especially enjoys exploring the outdoors...

and
nibbling on
dandelions,
clover,
leaves, and
some of my
delicious
garden
plantings.

After having her bottle and foraging, Tasha plays with us, boxes with her feet and runs around the yard. She enjoys being petted just like the dog and cats!

Tasha shows her affection by nibbling on my ear. All the animals enjoy warming by the fire.

Perhaps Tasha tells the cats about the wonder of the great outdoors - enticing nature stories, apparently, as Arthur keeps trying to escape to the outside.

We are sure, Arthur and Tasha are hoping no one will notice them on their outdoor foraging adventure.

Arthur, the cat, has been discovered outside and brought back indoors. Tasha must be very glad she is not an indoor cat. She can stay outside to explore and forage.

Sniff, sniff, nibble, nibble. And then it is time for another nap.

Tasha's life settles into a very comfortable routine of bottle feeding every 4 hours summoned by the sound of the bell.

We introduce new foods; grapes, apples, carrots, lettuce, and grain. But, Tasha much prefers the cats' food to her grain.

Tasha enjoys running around the yard at high speed.

Morgan often goes outside with Tasha - he just plunks down in the grass and watches Tasha run. He looks on in awe and perhaps thinks back to the days of his own youthful puppyhood.

Tasha has the companionship of the indoor
animals - but "plays" alone outside. She looks
longingly into the great wood beyond
the lush green yard.
Perhaps Tasha would like an outdoor playmate?
Another deer like herself?

Chapter Two. Tasha, My Story

The out of doors seems so very natural to me.

Is this where I truly belong?

I am growing. I notice that I am
much taller now than Morgan,
the dog. My spots
are getting lighter.
I spend much time outside
foraging for dandelion greens,
clover, apple leaves, and my
personal favorite,
day lily flowers.

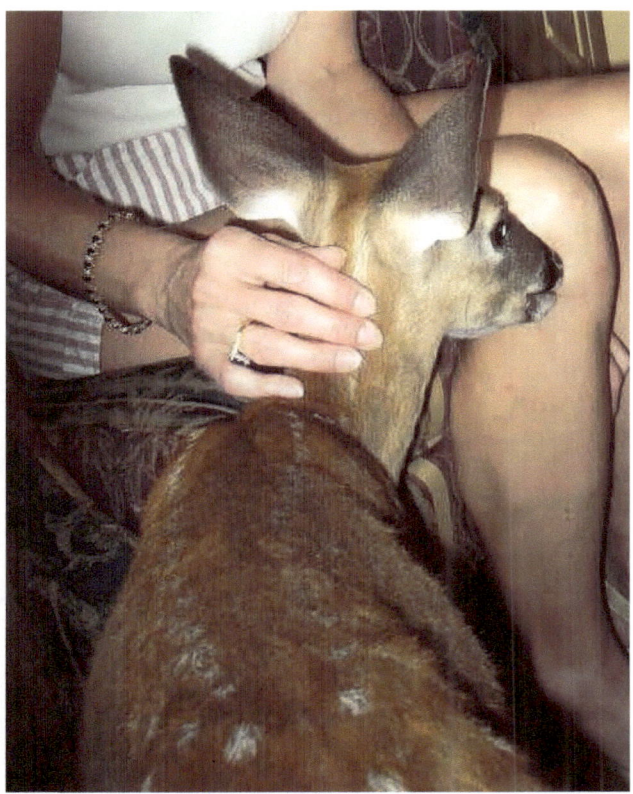

I still enjoy playing
with Morgan and
the cats,
but I am getting too
big and too fast to
"run around" in the
house.

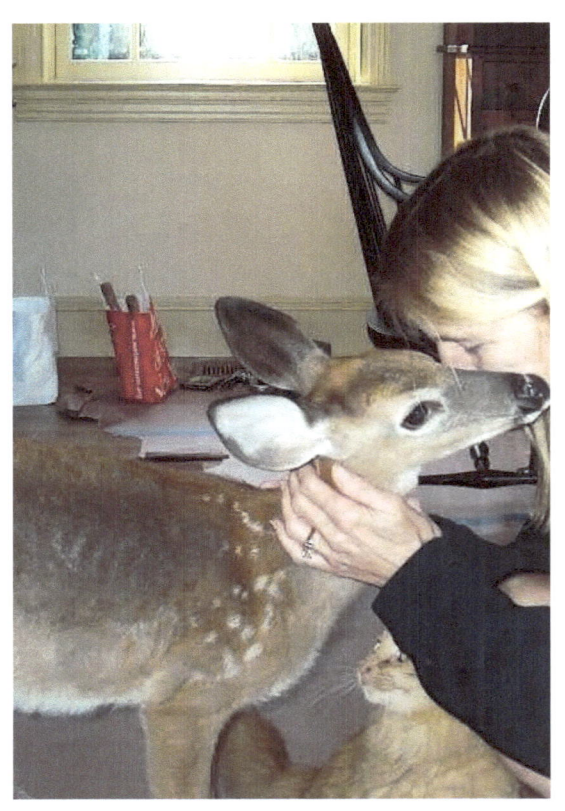

I spend most
of my day
outside
exploring,
further and
further into
the deep
woods.

Today in the
woods,
I encountered a
young fawn like
me with his
mother. The
young fawn and I
played, boxed and
foraged.

.

He showed me new
trails in the deep
wood and how to
drink out of the
stream. He talked
to me about
"danger".

At dusk, I return home, summoned by the ringing of the bell for my bottle, grain, treats and a good night's sleep with Morgan, Arthur, Avalon and Leo.

Could my new friends be my brother and my mother? I told them how I was rescued and taken into a family. I told them about cats and dog, and foods

like apples, carrots and grapes, and warm fires and comfortable beds. They showed me how to forage, to find shelter and survive in the deep woods. They welcomed me into the herd. Is this my new family?

I am so torn between my two worlds, my comfortable life with humans, Morgan, the dog and the cats and my bottle and treats and warm bed - and my very difficult life in nature with other deer like me.

Each day, I come back to my home while my deer mother and brother patiently wait for me at the edge of the wood. The warmth of the summer is waning and the bite of fall is in the air.

How can I leave the only home I really know? I grew up with Morgan and the cats...how can I go out into the wood to this strange new and dangerous life? Why would I want to? I have all the comforts any deer has ever known!!.....
That is it...that it is...I am a deer!!

Fall turns into the harsh reality and cold of winter. Foraging is the all consuming part of our lives as the lush green of summer becomes a memory.

I bring my herd close to the big house and tell them of
warm fires and plenty of food - delicious apples and
carrots and grapes - and comfortable warm bed.
I know I would still be welcome....

She loved and nurtured me and encouraged me to be true to my own nature. She let me go into the wild despite her love for me. That is true love.

This book is a must have for kids, especially those living in the city..the pictures are beautiful and the story line is clear and a success story! Sure to leave a lasting impression on a young mind and the adult reading it won't get at all drowsy :) Amazon Customer

Lovely and sweet story of Tasha. The first half is from the author's point of view, the other half from the deer's perspective. Good photography and a good learning experience for the little ones. Lcfriess

Lovely, cute and well written book. It's an original true story that's great for children. J. Rancourt

Beautiful story - perfect for all animal lovers both young and old... Jessica

Way to go!! This is a wonderful book for animal lovers of any age! P. Barone

www.ingramcontent.com/pod-product-compliance
Lightning Source LLC
Chambersburg PA
CBHW060815290526
45792CB00005BB/1667